SHAPING MODERN SCIENCE

What Is Atomic Theory?

Adam McLean

Crabtree Publishing Company

www.crabtreebooks.com

SHAPING MODERN SCIENCE

Author: Adam McLean

Publishing plan research and development:
Sean Charlebois, Reagan Miller
Crabtree Publishing Company

Editors: Sasha Patton, Adrianna Morganelli

Proofreaders: Gina Springer Shirley, Molly Aloian

Project coordinator: Kathy Middleton

Editorial services: Clarity Content Services

Production coordinator and prepress technician:
Katherine Berti

Print coordinator: Katherine Berti

Series consultant: Eric Walters

Cover design: Katherine Berti

Design: First Image

Photo research: Linda Tanaka

Illustrations: Adam McLean

Photographs: cover left David Parker/Photo Researchers, Inc.; cover top right and bottom right Shutterstock; title page Shutterstock; p4 Andrea Seemann/ Shutterstock; p5 Dariush M/Shutterstock; p6 oriontrail/ Shutterstock; p7 Maximilien Brice/CERN/The Atlas Experiment at CERN http://atlas.ch; p8 AntoinetteW/Shutterstock; p9 frog-traveller/Shutterstock; p10 Dmitri Kamenetsky/Shutterstock; p11 David H. Seymour/Shutterstock; p12 Simone Voigt/Shutterstock; p13 Detail of a paintingby Joseph Wright of Derby depicting the discovering of the element Phosphorus. CCL/wiki; p14 Public Domain/wiki; p15 Portrait of Monsieur de Lavoisier and his Wife, chemist Marie-Anne Pierrette Paulze, Metropolitan Museum of Art, N.Y. Public domain/wiki; p16 Frontispiece of John Dalton and the Rise of Modern Chemistry by Henry Roscoe, Public domain/wiki; p17 Magcom/Shutterstock; p21 Jonathunder/Public domain/wiki; p23 Inductiveload/NASA; p24 Michael Faraday in his laboratory at the Royal Institution. From a painting by Harriet Moore. The original is in the Chemical Heritage Foundation Collections, Public domain/wiki; p27 Ron Dale/Shutterstock; p28 Wolfe Larry/Shutterstock; p29 Alhovik/Shutterstock; p30 upper Valentyn Volkov/ Shutterstock; 2009fotofriends/Shutterstock; p33 Ernst Ruska Electron Microscope/Deutsches Museum Munich/J.Brew/Creative Commons Attribution-Share Alike 3.0 Unported License; p35 Library of Congress; p37 Public domain/wiki; p38 Public domain/wiki; p39 US Dept of Energy public domain; p40 Andrea Danti/Shutterstock; p41 US Dept of Energy/ Office of Public Affairs public domain; p42 US Dept of Energy public domain; p44 Tyler Boyes/Shutterstock; p45 NASA; p46 Kharkov Institute for Physics and Technology; p47 Moffett Studio/Library and Archives Canada/ C-017335; p48 US Dept of Energy; p49 Tyler Boyes/Shutterstock; p50 J. Pequenao/ CERN/The AtlasExperiment at CERN http://atlas.ch; p53 Maximilien Brice/CERN/The Atlas Experiment at CERN http://atlas.ch; p55 top Gonul Kokal/Shutterstock, JOANCHANG/Shutterstock; p56 ITER Organization; p57 The TMT Project is a collaboration of Caltech, University of California (UC) and the Association of Canadian Universities for Research in Astronomy (ACURA). © 2010 Thirty Meter Telescope.

Library and Archives Canada Cataloguing in Publication

McLean, Adam, 1977-
    What is atomic theory? / Adam McLean.

(Shaping modern science)
Includes index.
Issued also in electronic format.
ISBN 978-0-7787-7197-5 (bound).--ISBN 978-0-7787-7204-0 (pbk.)

    1. Atomic theory--Juvenile literature. I. Title. II. Series:
Shaping modern science

QD461.M34 2011   j541'.24   C2011-900174-8

Library of Congress Cataloging-in-Publication Data

McLean, Adam.
    What is atomic theory? / Adam McLean.
        p. cm. -- (Shaping modern science)
    Includes index.
    ISBN 978-0-7787-7197-5 (reinforced lib. bdg. : alk. paper) --
    ISBN 978-0-7787-7204-0 (pbk. : alk. paper) --
    ISBN 978-1-4271-9526-5 (electronic PDF)
    1. Atomic theory--Juvenile literature. 2. Dalton, John, 1766-
1844--Juvenile literature. I. Title. II. Series.

    QD461.M398 2011
    539.7--dc22
                                    2010052624

Crabtree Publishing Company

www.crabtreebooks.com   1-800-387-7650

Printed in the U.S.A./022011/CJ20101228

Copyright © **2011 CRABTREE PUBLISHING COMPANY.** All rights reserved. No part of this publication may be reproduced, stored in a retrieval system or be transmitted in any form or by any means, electronic, mechanical, photocopying, recording, or otherwise, without the prior written permission of Crabtree Publishing Company. In Canada: We acknowledge the financial support of the Government of Canada through the Canada Book Fund for our publishing activities.

Published in Canada
Crabtree Publishing
616 Welland Ave.
St. Catharines, ON
L2M 5V6

Published in the United States
Crabtree Publishing
PMB 59051
350 Fifth Avenue, 59th Floor
New York, New York 10118

Published in the United Kingdom
Crabtree Publishing
Maritime House
Basin Road North, Hove
BN41 1WR

Published in Australia
Crabtree Publishing
386 Mt. Alexander Rd.
Ascot Vale (Melbourne)
VIC 3032

Contents

What Is Atomic Theory?

One of the most exciting journeys in all of science has been the quest to imagine, observe, and understand **atoms**—the building blocks of matter within and around us. People have always wanted to see what their eyes cannot see by themselves, to explore what is too small to touch, and to use the energy stored in matter for the benefit of humankind.

Scientists have asked questions about matter, made hypotheses about its structure and function, and then tested those hypotheses by doing experiments. As a result, the theory of matter now describes everything from the tiniest amounts of elements and molecules, all the way up to entire planets, stars, and galaxies.

↑ *This giant statue of atoms joined together is found in Brussels, Belgium, and is called the Atomium.*

Scientific Theory or Law?

In science, a *theory* is a well-tested set of ideas that explains how something occurs. For example, many kinds of evidence together support Atomic Theory. A scientific *law* describes how something consistently happens under certain conditions. For example, the law of gravity describes how objects fall to Earth's surface.

In the current theory of matter, all substances—**solids**, **liquids**, **gases**, and other matter at the coldest and hottest temperatures in the universe—are made up of parts that are smaller than anyone can imagine. Think about it this way: the human body is made from organs, bones, muscles, and tendons. These are made from many types of cells that contain DNA and chemicals that power life. Similarly, matter is made from smaller and smaller components. These components act together in huge numbers to make materials that people can see, touch, smell, and taste.

The word *atom* is derived from the Greek word *atomos*, meaning "indivisible"—it is the basic unit of matter. There are so many atoms even in tiny objects like grains of sand that they can be counted only in powers of 10. Using powers of 10, the number of zeros in a big number can be shown as a single raised exponent of 10. For example, 100 is shown as 10^2 (10×10), 1,000 is 10^3 ($10 \times 10 \times 10$), and so on. If the number begins with something other than 1, then the power of 10 is multiplied by that number, so 500,000 would be 5×10^5. Using this method makes it easy to write big numbers in a small space. The number of atoms in an average grain of sand, for example, is 8×10^{19}. If that number was written out, it would be 80,000,000,000,000,000,000 (80 billion billion)!

How Many Atoms Are in That?

Approximately how many atoms are there in some everyday things? Here are some examples:

- an average-sized ant: 5×10^{20}
- a mechanical pencil: 1×10^{23}
- a small 8-ounce (227-g) milk carton: 2×10^{25}
- an average-sized laptop computer: 1×10^{26}
- 110 pounds (50 kg) of gold bars: 2×10^{26}
- one 110-pound (50-kg) person: 5×10^{27}
- the air inside a school classroom: 5×10^{27}
- an average-sized car: 1×10^{29}

↑ *This picture shows just a few atoms linked together as they would be in a solid material.*

"My goal is simple. It is a complete understanding of the universe, why it is as it is and why it exists at all."

—Stephen Hawking, English cosmologist and physicist (1942–)

Atoms, Atoms Everywhere!

Today, the properties of atoms are very well understood. Atomic theory describes the structure and function of matter. For example, it describes why diamond is the hardest material, while mercury—a metal unlike all other metals—is liquid at room temperature. Atomic theory also explains the nuclear forces that hold atoms together and electric forces that keep atoms apart. Studying these forces helps people understand chemical interactions—from those used in hair dye to those used in explosions—and the release and storage of energy such as in power plants, photosynthesis, and batteries.

From the Smallest to the Largest

Scientists who study atomic theory measure the size of atoms in billionths of an inch (which is the same as 0.000000001 inches), or billionths of a centimeter (0.000000001 cm). That's SMALL! At the other extreme, if the entire universe could be measured, including all of the stars in the sky from one side to the other, it would be nearly three billion billion billion feet (one billion billion billion meters) across, or 3 with 27 zeros after it (3,000,000,000,000,000,000,000,000,000 feet)! That's HUGE!

→ The size of people and objects that people interact with is just about in the middle between the tiny size of atoms, measured in billionths of an inch, and the billions and billions of miles between Earth and the stars in the sky.

"*The important thing is not to stop questioning. Curiosity has its own reason for existing. One cannot help but be in awe when contemplating the mysteries of eternity, of life, or the marvelous structure of reality. It is enough if one tries merely to comprehend a little of this mystery every day.*"

—Albert Einstein, German theoretical physicist (1879–1955)

→ *The largest atom smasher in the world is the Large Hadron Collider (LHC) in Europe. In it, particles collide at nearly the **speed of light** and break apart to reveal the smaller parts that atoms are made of.*

For over 4,000 years, people from all over the world have made contributions to atomic theory. The earliest ideas about matter were written down in ancient texts of India. From 600 B.C.–300 B.C., Greek philosophers imagined what matter was made of and what atoms might look like. In the eighteenth and nineteenth centuries, scientists experimented in chemistry and chemical interactions, leading to the modern use of cutting-edge technology and studies of nuclear physics. At times, atomic theory developed at a snail's pace—even appearing to go backward. At other times, though, especially in recent years, a lot has been learned about matter and energy very quickly.

Today, thousands of researchers on every continent study matter and the nature of the universe using atomic theory. For example, they make measurements at scales from the smallest particles to the largest planets, stars, and galaxies. They smash atoms together to probe what the atoms are made from, create new elements that are not found anywhere else in the universe, and use the most powerful computers in the world to learn about how the universe began.

CHAPTER ONE

Early Concepts About the World

What makes matter matter? This question has excited many great minds of science, as well as entire civilizations throughout history. The earliest people to write about a theory of matter were in India as far back as 2000 B.C., followed by Greek philosophers. During this time, there were no tools or technologies that could be used to study the atom. The nature of matter was closely linked to spiritual views about life, death, and the creation of the universe. The Rtam (Natural Law) in Indian sacred texts included the idea that a single element—water—was the origin of all matter. This idea came about independently in Greece by the philosophers Thales (who was born in 625 B.C. and died in 546 B.C.), known as the Father of Science; Anaximenes (585 B.C.–528 B.C.), who believed that air was the earliest element; and Heraclitus (535 B.C.–475 B.C.), known as the Weeping Philosopher, who thought that fire was first. Each believed mythology should not be needed in a scientific description of the world.

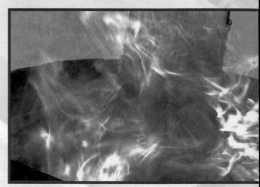

→ The first four elements were thought to be air, fire, earth, and water.

Ideas in Upanishadic texts of 900 B.C. in India, and ideas by the ancient Greek philosopher Empedocles (490 B.C.–430 B.C.) in 450 B.C., were combined into one theory that the universe was made from four elements: air, fire, earth, and water. Later, a fifth element that represented either another material (like metal) or matter that cannot be seen or touched (like space, the sky, or just a "force") was added by Aristotle (384 B.C.–322 B.C.). The same theory of matter with four or five base elements was later shared by different cultures all around the world: in fourth-century Sri Lanka, ninth-century Tibet, sixteenth-century Babylon, and seventeenth-century Japan.

Aristotle's Fifth Element: Ether

Aristotle believed that everything beyond the Moon was made with a pure, clear substance he called *quintessence* (where *quint* is the prefix for *five*, like the fifth element), or simply *ether*. He believed that the Sun, stars, and planets were all made from it, as well as the material in the space between them. This ether was where the gods of Greek mythology lived and what they breathed. Similarly, in ancient India, it was believed that elements in space were held in a material called *akasha*.

Since Greek times, scientists have found that the elements on the planets and stars are actually the same as those on Earth. Particles that are nearly impossible to detect do exist throughout the universe, but these particles are much smaller than Aristotle could have ever imagined!

↑ Greek philosopher Aristotle wrote, "In all things of nature there is something of the marvelous."

Origin of the Atom

The first major new idea in the theory of matter after Aristotle came from the Nyaya and Vaisheshika schools of philosophy in India, and the Greek philosopher Democritus (460 B.C.–370 B.C.) and his mentor, Leucippus (his dates of birth and death are unknown). They suggested that all matter was made up of tiny solid particles called atoms that could not be seen or separated, and that they were always in motion. These philosophers believed that atoms could not be changed or destroyed, and that properties like color and flavor were part of each type of atom. This theory was known as **atomism**, and was very controversial at a time when Greek people believed their lives were controlled by gods living on Mount Olympus. Democritus argued that all matter must be made from small components because all things grow, change, and decay. He observed that even the hardest rock was eroded by drops of water over time.

↑ *Erosion of rock at a shoreline like this takes place ov[er] thousands of years.*

"Nothing happens at random, but everything for a reason and by necessity."

—Leucippus, fifth century B.C.

Quick fact

Democritus wrote over 60 books and texts in his lifetime. He believed that the highest goal in life was cheerfulness, and because of that, he was known as the Laughing Philosopher. Maybe Democritus was right, since an average person during his lifetime lived to be only about 40 years old, and Democritus lived to be nearly 100!

Many philosophers at the time disagreed strongly with Democritus; especially Aristotle, who was very influential. Aristotle believed that matter in each of the five elements was continuous and not made from atoms that could not be seen. Because of his influence, Aristotle's ideas stayed popular into the Middle Ages, but atomism did not disappear. One of the key works that continued the idea of atomism into modern times was an epic poem written by the Roman Lucretius (99 B.C.–55 B.C.).

In his poem, "On the Nature of Things," Lucretius attempted to convince the ruling magistrate and the people of Rome that everything was made from atoms and controlled not by gods but by laws of nature. He used the principles of atomism to discuss philosophy; life and death; a theory of human senses; the origin of the world; seasons; heavenly bodies; and natural events like storms, earthquakes, and volcanoes. Unfortunately, the poem did not convince the magistrate that forces other than those of gods controlled the Sun, the stars, and the rest of the natural world. But the poem did help atomism continue until scientists discovered that atoms did truly exist.

↑ The Parthenon was built in Athens, Greece, in 438 B.C., as a temple for the goddess Athena, who was thought to be the protector of the city.

"It's the right idea, but not the right time."

—John Dalton (1766–1844)

The Study of Alchemy

From 700 A.D. through the Middle Ages, and even to the present, there has been a fascination with attempting to change one material into another. Some scientists were especially interested in changing common materials like iron, nickel, lead, and zinc into rare, expensive metals like gold. This practice was called **alchemy**. Followers believed that the success of alchemy would lead to wisdom and immortality (to live forever)! Although it was not successful, many well known scientists practiced alchemy, including Sir Isaac Newton (1643–1727) who described gravity, and Robert Boyle (1629–1691) who was known as the first modern chemist. The practice of alchemy did, however, lead the way to modern chemistry and more advanced experimental principles.

←The mortar (bowl) and pestle (pounder) have been used by alchemists and chemists to grind and mix substances since they were invented in Mexico more than 5,000 years ago.

The Role of the Alchemists

Ancient alchemists were not able to create gold from other metals, but alchemists did help the study of chemistry. They also helped in other surprising areas. In Egypt, as far back as 5000 B.C., early alchemists created the process of mummification. In 1200 B.C., alchemists in India studied metals so they could be used as money, ornaments, and weapons. In China, beginning in the second century, alchemists worked mostly on developing medicines called elixirs from common substances, many of which are still used today. In 800 A.D., alchemists in Persia (the modern Middle East) even tried to create artificial life! In the Middle Ages (after 1300 A.D.), alchemists in Europe were a big inspiration for art and stories.

Alchemy had an even greater role in modern science: helping to develop the scientific method. By the seventeenth century, alchemy was thought to be a very serious form of science. Experiments including recipes with many strange ingredients and dozens of exact steps—sometimes lasting for many days—were done very carefully. Alchemists did this to make sure they did not miss any chance that small amounts of gold or other desirable elements were created. They also wanted to reduce the risk of explosions when unstable chemicals were made! Finally, it was through the study of alchemy that the element phosphorus was discovered in 1669. Phosphorus is toxic, and it glows in the dark in contact with air.

↑Hennig Brand is pictured in his lab during the discovery of phosphorus. Look at it glow!

"There is nothing like looking, if you want to find something. You certainly usually find something, if you look, but it is not always quite the something you were after."

—J.R.R. Tolkien, *The Lord of the Rings*

Quick fact

Sometimes, science is smelly! In 1669 in Germany, the alchemist Hennig Brand used almost 1,500 gallons (5,500 L) of urine to create just four ounces (120 g) of phosphorus! Urine contains phosphate molecules, which he isolated and heated until they burst into flames, leaving a liquid that hardened and glowed green—phosphorus!

Joining Atoms Together

One of the most famous alchemists was English chemist and philosopher Robert Boyle. Boyle's broad background in alchemy and the careful methods he used to carry out his experiments led him to publish a book called *The Sceptical Chymist,* in 1680. In his book, Boyle presented his ideas that matter is made of atoms that could combine together to form molecules and chemical compounds. He also believed that the molecules and chemical compounds may have very different properties than the basic atomic elements used to form them. His experiments demonstrated that collisions between chemicals and their reactions to each other were the basis of all matter. Through his work, Boyle discovered compounds made from copper and mercury. He also discovered many new reactions with strong acids, and was the first to isolate and describe the lightest element, called hydrogen. He asked chemists to think beyond the philosophical roots of alchemy and ancient ideas that the elements are limited to air, fire, earth, and water.

↑ *Robert Boyle was known as the skeptical chemist.*

Quick fact

Robert Boyle founded the Royal Society of London for the Improvement of Natural Knowledge in 1660. The society still exists today and is the oldest continuous scientific society in the world!

After Boyle came new discoveries in chemistry about how chemicals combined. Joseph Proust (1754–1826) was a French chemist who discovered the law of definite proportions, also known as Proust's Law. This law states that chemical compounds always have the same fraction of each element in them by mass. For example, in water—known by its chemical structure H_2O—there are always two units of hydrogen to one unit of oxygen, no matter how much water is present.

Antoine-Laurent de Lavoisier (1743–1794), created the first law of the conservation of mass. This law states that the mass of ingredients (or reactants) put into a chemical reaction, and the products of that reaction, must be equal. These important observations and other advancements—like adding to the list of known elements and creating a standard system for expressing chemical reactions in writing—helped make atomic theory understandable to scientists through to the nineteenth century.

Did You Know?

In addition to being a brilliant scientist, Antoine-Laurent de Lavoisier was a very wealthy tax collector in France. When the Reign of Terror started during the French Revolution (1789–1799), he was falsely accused of being a traitor and was executed by guillotine in 1794.

←Antoine-Laurent de Lavoisier and his wife, Marie-Anne Pierrette Paulze (1758–1836), worked side-by-side in their laboratory. Paulze was very important in the work, especially in translation, illustration of scientific papers, and publication of the results.

CHAPTER TWO

Atomic Theory Takes Shape

By the turn of the nineteenth century, the theory of matter had come a very long way. Early chemists had observed that atoms interacted together according to laws that could be written down and tested. By 1800, 36 separate elements had been discovered, but most people still believed that these elements were made from the five base elements. The groundwork was set for future scientists to use the scientific method to experiment with new elements and new models for the atom, then write down and discuss their results.

In 1802, John Dalton (1766–1844) combined many of the ideas discovered so far about atoms, as well as his own research, into a single atomic theory known as Dalton's Atomic Theory.

↑ John Dalton put together the first atomic theory.

Quick fact

In addition to his study of atomic theory, Dalton studied weather. He kept daily weather records for 57 years, totaling over 200,000 measurements! Unfortunately, his work was lost during World War II, which prompted a famous scientist of the time, Isaac Asimov (1920–1992), to say, "It is not only the living who are killed in war."

"Only those who dare to fail greatly can ever achieve greatly."

—Robert F. Kennedy (1925–1968)

Dalton's Atomic Theory

Dalton's Atomic Theory included these principles:

1. All matter is composed of atoms.
2. Atoms cannot be created, destroyed, or separated into smaller particles.
3. All atoms of a given element are the same.
4. Different elements have different types of atoms, and they can be identified by their atomic weight.
5. Atoms of one element can combine with atoms of another element into chemical compounds with the same fraction of each type of atom.

Dalton added another point: atoms would almost always combine in pairs, as a binary compound. He could not prove this point, though. As a result, he predicted that the chemical formula for water was HO, not H_2O, but he was wrong! He also predicted the wrong weights for oxygen (O) and nitrogen (N). While these mistakes prevented his theory from being fully accepted, most of his first five points have stood firm even until today.

Until very late in the 1800s, scientists were sure that atoms were solid and could not be separated into smaller parts. This belief changed in 1897 when Joseph John "J.J." Thomson (1856–1940) discovered the **electron**. Many advancements in the field of electricity in the eighteenth and nineteenth centuries made this discovery possible.

Since electricity was now well known, scientists who were interested in atomic theory were able to use an electrical conductor called the **cathode** to study **electric charge**.

In the 1870s, William Crookes (1832–1919) invented the first high-quality cathode ray tube. In it, the air had been removed from a glass chamber, so particles could travel through the tube without being blocked. A phosphorus coating was applied to the side of the tube opposite the cathode. Finally, an X-shaped mask was inserted to block the way of particles given off by the cathode. When an electric field was present, electrons were released from the cathode and traveled to the phosphorus, which glowed by a process called fluorescence. A shadow was left where the mask was in the way of the electrons.

First Piece of the Atomic Puzzle

In the late 1890s, J.J. Thomson studied the rays of light produced by a cathode. He found that they could be shifted (or deflected) by an electric field, and the combination of an electric and magnetic field. By measuring the size of the deflection, he was able to measure the mass of one of the electrons in the rays. He found it was about 2,000 times less than the mass of hydrogen, the lightest atom! Thomson had discovered the electron, the negatively charged particle that was produced in a beam by the cathode.

The Cathode Ray Tube

Crookes' low pressure (or vacuum) cathode ray tube (or CRT) would be improved by German physicists Johann Hittorf (1824–1914) and Eugen Goldstein (1850–1930), American Thomas Edison (1847–1931), and German Karl Ferdinand Braun (1850–1918) in 1897. In 1907, Braun's CRT was then used by Russian scientist Boris Rosing (1869–1933) to create a video image. And with that, the original television was born!

↑*Crookes' cathode ray tube is shown with an electric current flowing through it.*

Different types of Crookes' cathode tubes also led to the invention of the neon light by Nikola Tesla (1856–1943) in 1893 and the fluorescent lamp by Thomas Edison in 1896. Crookes' CRT was also used to invent the vacuum tube electric amplifier by American Lee de Forest (1873–1961) in 1906, which was used in the first radio and television broadcast, radar, telephone networks, and the first computers.

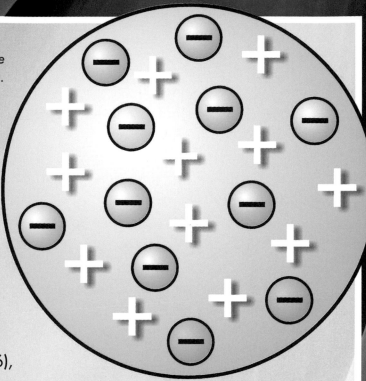

→ *J.J. Thomson suggested the "plum pudding" model of the atom.*

Thanks to Thomson's discovery of the electron, it was now known that the atom was not a solid object. So what form did it take? Many scientists in the early 1900s had different ideas:

- In 1902, the cubical model of the atom was suggested by American chemist Gilbert Lewis (1875–1946), and refined by Irving Langmuir (1881–1957) in 1919. In this model, atoms were in the shape of a cube, and electrons were found at the corners. Compounds were formed by electrons at one, two, three, or four corners of two cubes joining together.

- In 1904, J.J. Thomson suggested that atoms were made of a positively charged soup with electrons found inside in rotating rings. This "plum-pudding" model looked like a popular dessert at the time.

- Also in 1904, Japanese physicist Hantaro Nagaoka (1865–1950) suggested the Saturnian model. In this model, electrons revolved around a central core in a ring, like the rings of the planet Saturn.

With the pros and cons of these models in mind, physicist Ernest Rutherford (1871–1937) from New Zealand, with the help of Hans Geiger (1882–1945) and Ernest Marsden (1889–1970), performed an experiment that would lead to the winning theory. The experiment used radium, which was known to release small atoms in all directions called **alpha particles**. Alpha particles had the same mass as helium atoms but with a lot more energy.

"The whole of science is nothing more than a refinement of everyday thinking."

—Albert Einstein

What Did an Atom Look Like?

A detector was made from zinc sulfide (ZnS), which lit up when it was struck by the particles that were released from radium. When the particles were aimed at a gold (Au) sheet, most particles went straight through the sheet. Some alpha particles, however, caused the detector to light up on the same side of the sheet as the radium source! This meant that the particles must have been reflected off something very hard and very small in the gold. In a paper published in 1911, Rutherford suggested the planetary model of the atom. In this model, electrons orbited not in a ring but as a cloud around a central core or **nucleus**. With this experiment, the idea of an atomic nucleus was proven!

Two years later, in 1913, Danish physicist Niels Bohr (1885–1962) added the idea that electric fields between negatively charged electrons and a positively charged nucleus must hold electrons in their orbits. He thought that electrons could circle at different orbit levels above the nucleus depending on how much energy they had. When electrons jumped to lower levels, Bohr suggested that energy would be released as light. This part of the Bohr model of the atom explained another observation: the release of specific colors of light when hydrogen was burned.

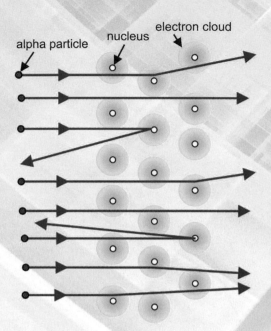

↑ *Rutherford's use of alpha particles proved that the nucleus existed.*

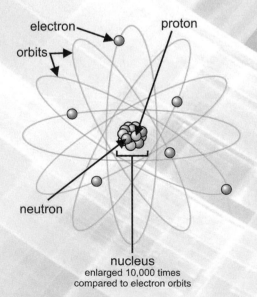

nucleus
enlarged 10,000 times
compared to electron orbits

↑ *Rutherford's and Bohr's experiments suggested this model of the atom.*

Following the discoveries of the electron and nucleus, Dutch physicist Antonius van den Broek (1870–1926) recognized that each element had a different nuclear charge opposite to that of the negative electron. This was confirmed first in 1913 by Henry Moseley (1887–1915) of Britain using **X-rays**. In 1919, Rutherford proved that the nucleus of hydrogen was found in other elements when he directed alpha particles into nitrogen gas (N_2). Because a hydrogen nucleus had a positive charge of only one, and the positive charges of other nuclei were greater, he suggested that there was an elementary particle of positive charge in the nucleus. Rutherford named this particle the **proton**.

↑ *The Nobel Prize medal is 2.6 inches (6.6 cm) in diameter and made from 6.2 ounces (175 g) of solid gold.*

The final part of the atom to be discovered was found to exist in the nucleus with the proton. In 1931, an experiment by German physicist Walther Bothe (1891–1957) and his student Herbert Becker showed that particles not affected by a magnetic field were produced by hitting light elements lithium (Li), boron (B), and beryllium (Be) with alpha particles. In 1932, James Chadwick (1891–1974) of England found that the new particle had about the same mass as a hydrogen atom—much heavier than the electron. Chadwick had discovered the **neutron**, and he won the Nobel Prize in Physics in 1935.

A picture of the classical structure of an atom was now complete.

CHAPTER THREE

Photons, Electrons, and the Nucleus

In 1900, a German physicist named Max Planck (1858–1947) was studying how to get the most light out of a lightbulb. He noticed that light was released by heat sources like the hot filament of a bulb. He also noticed that the light was released in a particular pattern of frequencies for different materials. Each frequency of light corresponded to different colors of light seen by the eye. These frequencies followed the colors of the rainbow: red at the lowest frequency, orange, yellow, green, blue, purple, and finally violet at the highest frequency. Planck theorized that the only way this could happen was if light came in packets of energy. In 1905, German theoretical physicist Albert Einstein (1879–1955) named these packets of light energy **photons**. He described how they could be treated as either particles or as waves—like waves traveling across an ocean.

Bohr's model of the atom included a way to understand how different colors of light were emitted from atoms when they were excited by energy. When a material is heated, the atoms within it gain energy and move up and down, and side to side, colliding with the atoms beside it and transmitting energy. This transfer of energy causes the electrons in the atom to jump up to a higher energy level; that is, a higher orbit around the atom. After some time, the electron drops back down to the lower energy level, releasing the energy it gained in a specific amount.

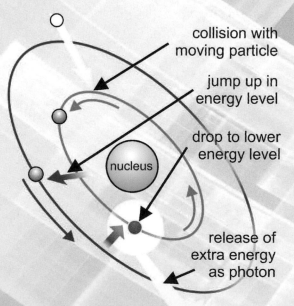

collision with moving particle

jump up in energy level

drop to lower energy level

nucleus

release of extra energy as photon

The understanding that light was released in various frequencies that corresponded to different colors was later found to apply to many types of waves that were known to travel as photons. These were assembled together in a complete series called the **electromagnetic spectrum**, which included the spectrum of visible light in one small portion near the center.

The spectrum linked photons of many types, each with specific wavelengths and different effects on matter as they collided. These photons included radio waves at the lowest frequency (and least energy), microwaves, infrared light, visible light, ultraviolet light, X-rays, and very high-energy **gamma rays** at the highest frequency (and most energy).

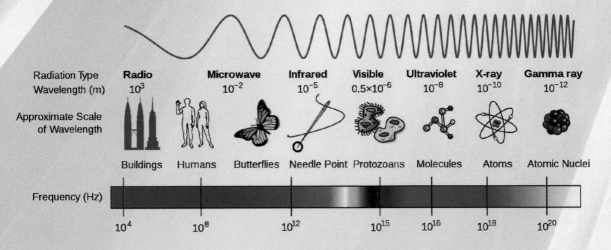

Radiation Type	Radio	Microwave	Infrared	Visible	Ultraviolet	X-ray	Gamma ray
Wavelength (m)	10^3	10^{-2}	10^{-5}	$0.5×10^{-6}$	10^{-8}	10^{-10}	10^{-12}
Approximate Scale of Wavelength	Buildings	Humans	Butterflies	Needle Point	Protozoans	Molecules	Atoms	Atomic Nuclei

Frequency (Hz)						
10^4	10^8	10^{12}	10^{15}	10^{16}	10^{18}	10^{20}

↑ The electromagnetic spectrum includes photons of all frequencies, including many that are used every day.

"All things are made of atoms—little particles that move around in perpetual motion, attracting each other when they are a little distance apart, but repelling upon being squeezed into one another. In that sentence. . .there is an enormous amount of information about the world."

—Richard P. Feynman, *Six Easy Pieces: Essentials of Physics By Its Most Brilliant Teacher* (1995)

More Discoveries in Atomic Theory

Starting in 1839, an English physicist named Michael Faraday (1791–1867) demonstrated important connections between electricity and magnetism that would later help people understand how atomic theory is connected to light. He first showed that by wrapping one wire into a tight coil around another wire, and flowing newly discovered electrons through one wire, an electric current could be generated in the other wire. This experiment was repeated using a fast-moving magnet through the coil.

Faraday showed that a moving magnetic field could bring about an electric field. He created a theory that electric and magnetic fields were connected—as electromagnetism—and they extended beyond conductors and magnets into the space around them. Faraday's discoveries proved that energy transmitted as light was related to electromagnetic fields. This was very important for understanding future experiments that would show that light could act as a particle, or sometimes as a wave.

↑Michael Faraday is shown in his lab around 1850. Here, Faraday invented an early version of the Bunsen burner and discovered electrolysis—splitting water molecules with electricity.

New discoveries and ways to arrange the atoms of different elements into one ordered set were helping bring atomic theory forward as well. Since the mass and electric charge of many elements were now known, symbols for two separate counting systems were used to list the elements. The first was the atomic mass, A, equal to the sum of the number of protons and the number of neutrons in its nucleus. The second was the atomic number, Z. Z tells the number of protons in the nucleus of an atom alone. The number of neutrons in an atom's nucleus is also given a name, the neutron number, N. For an atom, then, $A = N + Z$.

Surprisingly, the number of neutrons in the nucleus of one element can be different. In 1913, J.J. Thomson discovered the first example of this. He found that natural neon was a combination of atoms with 10 neutrons ($N = 10$, $A = 20$) and atoms with 12 neutrons ($N = 12$, $A = 22$). In both cases, though, $Z = 10$. Later that year, Scottish doctor Margaret Todd (1859–1918) named different forms of the same atom **isotopes**. In total, there are 3,100 isotopes known today!

What's in a Nucleus?

For most light elements, the number of neutrons and protons in the nucleus is equal.

Helium (He): $A = N + Z$
$$4 = 2 + 2$$

As elements get heavier, the number of neutrons in the nucleus increases faster than the number of protons.

Uranium (Ur): $A = N + Z$
$$240 = 146 + 94$$

That's 55 percent more neutrons than protons!

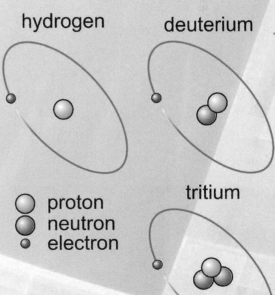

hydrogen   deuterium

tritium

proton
neutron
electron

→ *The atomic structure of all three isotopes of hydrogen are shown. For most elements, there is one primary isotope that makes up the majority of atoms of that element in the world (and universe).*

Arranging the Elements in a Table

Thirty-six elements were discovered before 1800. Twenty-two new elements were discovered between 1800 and 1849, and 23 additional elements between 1850 and 1899. As early as 1829, scientists had recognized that the chemical properties of lighter elements followed patterns that could be grouped together. German chemist Johann Wolfgang Döbereiner (1780–1849) was the first to do so. He found groups of three elements that he called triads, in which the average mass of the first and last elements equaled that of the middle element (for example, chlorine, bromine, and iodine—all of which are very reactive with water).

The Mass of an Atom in Perspective

Democritus had no idea just how small atoms were! We can now measure the mass of the parts of an atom with extreme accuracy.

- Mass of an electron: 3.21×10^{-29} ounces (9.11×10^{-31} kg)
- Mass of a proton: 5.90×10^{-26} ounces (1.67×10^{-27} kg), or 1,836 times more than an electron
- Mass of a neutron: 5.91×10^{-26} ounces (1.675×10^{-27} kg), or 1,838 times more than an electron

To put this in perspective, if the mass of an electron was magnified to be equal to the mass of an average-sized apple (⅓ pound, or 150 g), a proton or neutron would have a mass of over 600 pounds (275 kg)!

"Atoms are mainly empty space. Matter is composed chiefly of nothing."

—Carl Sagan (*Cosmos: A Personal Voyage*)

Quick fact

In terms of volume, an atom including the nucleus and electrons is 99.9999999999986 percent empty space! If all of that empty space could be filled, matter could be squished nearly 100 trillion times!

In 1862, French geologist Alexandre-Emile Béguyer de Chancourtois (1820–1886) was the first to notice that elements with similar properties occurred in intervals when ordered by their atomic weight. In 1865, English chemist John Newlands created a table to predict that a new element existed—germanium (Ge, Z = 32). In 1864, chemists William Odling (1829–1921) of England, Lothar Meyer (1830–1895) of Germany, and Dmitri Mendeleev (1834–1907) of Russia worked independently on finding a good way to organize atoms. Mendeleev did the best job by including all of the known elements and predicting the existence of three elements that had not yet been discovered. His table became known as the **periodic table** of the elements.

Thanks to the periodic table and more advanced technology, the final 13 natural elements were found from 1900 to 1949, bringing the total to 94. From 1950 onward, scientists figured out how to create new elements not found anywhere else in the universe. As a result, the periodic table today has 118 elements on it!

Periodic table of the chemical elements

The current standard table contains 117 elements as of March 10, 2009 (elements 1-116 and element 118).

Li	Alkali metals	
Be	Alkaline earth metals	
La	Lanthanides	
Ac	Actinides	
Sc	Transition elements	
Al	Other metals	
B	Metalloids	
H	Other nonmetals	
F	Halogens	
He	Noble gases	

CHAPTER FOUR

Elements, Properties, and Chemical Reactions

Though they are small, electrons are the glue that can join one atom to another. The chemical properties of each element and groups of elements are determined by the way the electrons in one atom interact with electrons of other atoms nearby. Most physical properties of matter like density, shape, and texture are also determined by interactions between electrons. Other properties like a material's color are determined by how an atom's electrons absorb or reflect particles of light. Considering all that the electron does, it's hard to believe that it is 2,000 times smaller than either the proton or the neutron!

When two or more elements are added together, they will do one of two things: mix or combine. When two elements mix together, no change in their structure occurs. In a mixture of sand and water, for example, atoms of each material collide with one another to make mud, but they stay chemically separate. The sand and the water mixture can be separated back out. Air is a mixture of 80 percent nitrogen and 19 percent oxygen, plus many other gases to make up the rest. The properties of the mixture are the same as the properties of each of its components.

When two or more atoms combine together in a chemical reaction, the result is called a chemical compound. A compound is held together by a chemical bond with a specific structure. Compounds held together by forces between atoms in the structure are called molecules. Once together, compounds can only be separated chemically using energy. Compounds can have very different properties than the individual elements that were combined to make them. Compounds can be simple, like water (H_2O), or complex, like a sugar molecule ($C_6H_{12}O_6$).

Atoms Joining Together

Most atoms on the periodic table exist in nature not as elements, but as compounds—two or more elements joined together. There are two types of chemical bonds: primary, which are strong connections between elements that form molecules, and secondary, which are weak connections between compounds.

The primary bonds are ionic, covalent, and metallic. **Ionic bonds** are made between one metal and one nonmetal, like sodium chloride (NaCl), also called table salt. An electron from one element is given to another element, making the first atom positively charged and the second atom negatively charged. **Covalent bonds** were discovered in 1919 by Irving Langmuir. They are made between two nonmetals when they share pairs of electrons, like in hydrogen gas (H_2) and hydrochloric acid (HCl). In a covalent bond, the electrons are sometimes with one atom, then sometimes with the other. In a **metallic bond**, like in iron (Fe, Z=26) and gold (Au, Z=79), the electron in the highest energy orbit around an atom is shared between atoms, but not held strongly. The shared electrons are able to move between atoms freely. This makes metals very good at transmitting heat and electricity.

Secondary bonds take place between hydrogen atoms in separate molecules, and in large compounds. In a hydrogen bond, like between water (H_2O) molecules, the shared electrons leave hydrogen with a slightly positive charge, and the other element is slightly negative, which makes the separate molecules attract. In large compounds, non-covalent bonds can cause shifting of electron clouds. These bonds are important for the three-dimensional structure of complicated molecules, like DNA.

Quick fact

If all the elements in a human body could be separated, they could be purchased in a chemical supply store for about $1 in total!

States of Matter

Matter exists in four basic states, or phases: solid, liquid, gas, and **plasma**. In a solid, atoms are held together tightly. The structure of the atoms in a solid can be organized into a three-dimensional pattern called a lattice, like in diamond, or disorganized but still held together, like in glass. The molecules of liquids are held together, but not as tightly as in a solid. This weak connection allows a liquid to flow, but does not let a liquid expand into the space it is in, or allow it to be easily compressed. In a gas, molecules have weak forces between them and are able to move apart freely. This allows a gas to fill the space it is found in. Finally, in a plasma, atoms are so energetic that they overcome the forces that keep the electrons connected to the nucleus of the atom. Therefore, negatively charged electrons and positively charged nuclei are separated. Plasmas exist only at very high temperatures, about 21,200 degrees Fahrenheit (10,000°C) or more.

↑ *Three states of matter are shown at once: two solids, a liquid, and many gases.*

→ *Some common examples of plasmas include the gas inside a fluorescent lightbulb, stars, or air when a bolt of lightning strikes.*

Every element or compound can exist in every state of matter. The state that a material is in depends on how much energy it has. More energy means atoms and molecules move farther apart and usually become less dense. Less energy means atoms and molecules move more slowly, come closer together, and usually become denser. When one state of matter changes into another, it is called a phase change or phase transition. For example, adding energy to H_2O molecules and changing their structure from ice to water is an example of melting. In the opposite direction, energy is removed and the water freezes into ice. Once H_2O is in the liquid state, adding more energy will eventually cause it to boil and become steam or vapor—a gas.

Cooling the steam will cause it to condense back to a liquid—water. When H_2O is at very low temperatures and pressures, and energy is added, solid ice can also change directly into a vapor. This process is called sublimation, and it occurs in freeze-drying. It also happens to glaciers. Vapor can also change directly back to ice. This process is called deposition, and it occurs when snow is formed in clouds, and when frost forms on the ground. Finally, the transition to a plasma occurs only when a gas is super-heated and its atoms lose their electrons. This process is called ionization, while the reverse—the removal of energy to form a gas from a plasma—is called deionization.

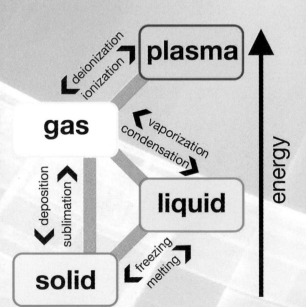

←All of the processes that change one state of matter to another are shown.

Temperature and Matter in Motion

In physics, the temperature of matter is a measure of the amount of moving energy, or kinetic energy, that atoms of matter carry with them as they move. Kinetic energy was first described in 1829 by French scientist Gaspard-Gustave Coriolis (1792–1843). Knowing that temperature is a measure of moving energy, the lowest temperature possible would be when all matter—including atoms themselves—stop moving. In 1848, Irish physicist Lord Kelvin (1824–1907) used a mathematical definition of heat figured out by James Joule (1818–1889) to define the lowest possible temperature of matter, equal to –459.67 degrees Fahrenheit (–273.15°C).

This temperature is called absolute zero—no lower temperature is possible anywhere in the universe. So far, it has been possible to bring matter only very close to this temperature.

On the other hand, there is almost no limit to the highest temperature of matter. Tungsten, for example, melts at 6,170 degrees Fahrenheit (3,410°C). The center of the Sun is estimated to be 27 million degrees Fahrenheit (15 million degrees Celsius). A supernova—the death of a star— is estimated to take place at 212 billion degrees Fahrenheit (100 billion degrees Celsius)!

Temperatures in a Laboratory

The lowest temperature ever achieved in a laboratory is –459.66999999982 degrees Fahrenheit (–273.1499999999°C)! This was done using very strong magnetic fields to slow atoms of rhodium (Rh, Z=45) almost to a complete stop!

The highest temperature ever measured in a laboratory is 6.6 billion degrees Fahrenheit (3.7 billion degrees Celsius)!

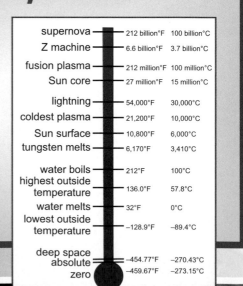

supernova	212 billion°F	100 billion°C
Z machine	6.6 billion°F	3.7 billion°C
fusion plasma	212 million°F	100 million°C
Sun core	27 million°F	15 million°C
lightning	54,000°F	30,000°C
coldest plasma	21,200°F	10,000°C
Sun surface	10,800°F	6,000°C
tungsten melts	6,170°F	3,410°C
water boils	212°F	100°C
highest outside temperature	136.0°F	57.8°C
water melts	32°F	0°C
lowest outside temperature	–128.9°F	–89.4°C
deep space	–454.77°F	–270.43°C
absolute zero	–459.67°F	–273.15°C

Atoms are in constant motion at all temperatures above absolute zero, no matter what state of matter they are in. In 60 B.C., Lucretius first suggested that atoms were in motion, which he wrote about in his poem "On the Nature of Things." He noticed sunbeams lighting up tiny dust particles which moved in all directions in the air. He thought their motion meant that matter was constantly moving, but that motion normally couldn't be seen. In 1784, the same random motion was recognized by Dutch chemist Jan Ingenhousz (1730–1799) (who also discovered photosynthesis!) when he observed black charcoal dust floating on the surface of alcohol. In 1827, Scottish botanist Robert Brown (1773–1858) also described a similar motion of flower pollen in water viewed under a microscope. Today the movement of gases is named Brownian motion.

↑ The electron microscope was invented in 1931 by German physicist Ernst Ruska (1906–1988) and engineer Max Knoll (1897–1969).

In 1889, Louis Georges Gouy (1854–1926) of France found that Brownian motion was faster for smaller gas molecules and smaller particles (this is why large objects do not show similar motion). In 1900, Austrian meteorologist Felix Maria Exner (1876–1930) measured how the speed of the motion depended on both particle size and temperature. This observation was, in 1905, explained by Albert Einstein. Brownian motion was first observed in liquids in 1992 using an electron microscope, and in solid crystals in 1995.

"Research is what I'm doing when I don't know what I'm doing."

—Wernher von Braun, German-American rocket scientist

CHAPTER FIVE

Rays and Radiation

Most matter that people interact with from day to day is stable—its structure and mass do not change with time. The nuclei of some atoms, though, can become unstable if, for example, they collide with another particle, or if they gain a lot of energy. When the nucleus of an atom becomes unstable, it reacts by releasing particles and energy from the nucleus in order to become stable again. This process is called **radiation**, and the unstable material is described as radioactive. The term *radiation* is from the root word *radiate*, meaning "to send out waves or particles away from the source."

There are two main types of radiation: ionizing and nonionizing. When ionizing radiation from one atom interacts with another atom with enough energy, the second atom may lose one of its orbiting electrons. This leaves the second atom with a positive charge, which is called an **ion**. This means it may chemically react with other atoms in ways that it would not if the radiation were not there. Because of this effect, ionizing radiation can be damaging to sensitive living cells. In significant quantities, it may cause burns, or cancer over a long period of time. The other type of radiation, nonionizing, does not have enough energy to remove electrons from other atoms.

Quick fact

Every one of the 50 trillion living cells in the human body experiences over 100,000 changes in its DNA per day! These changes are due to errors in normal replication, chemical decay, infection, and exposure to ionizing radiation. If the cell is not fixed, it may lead to mutations or cancer, but fortunately, DNA is fantastic at fixing itself! Over 99.99999 percent of all changes in DNA structure are repaired without a person even knowing!

"Not only is the universe stranger than we imagine, it is stranger than we can imagine."

—Albert Einstein

Radiation has existed since Earth began over four billion years ago. Much of the rock and gases that formed our planet were unstable at that time. Most of that matter has become stable, but some remains in the ground, in the air, and in the water. Some new radioactive material is made by natural processes, and some is made by humans. Because of this, all life receives a background level of radiation every year. Living beings have adapted to cope with this level of radiation by repairing the damage when it happens or by having another cell replace the damaged one.

Radiation was first discovered by French physicist Antoine-Henri Becquerel (1852–1908) in 1896. He was planning to study exposure of photographic plates in the sunlight using fluorescent material. To do so, he wrapped the fluorescent material in the plates along with a dense salt of uranium. Even before bringing the plates into the Sun, though, an image of the substance was already found on the plates. The reason, he concluded, was that particles of light must have been emitted from the salt to expose the plates.

←Antoine-Henri Becquerel shared the 1903 Nobel Prize in Physics with Marie and Pierre Curie for their discovery of **radioactivity**.

Radiation Is Everywhere!

Background Radiation

The effect of radiation on living things is commonly measured in the unit of sieverts, named after Swedish medical physicist Rolf Sievert (1896–1966). Sievert was one of the first scientists to study the biological effects of radiation. An average person in the United States receives 3.6 millisieverts of radiation each year, so about 10 microsieverts per day.

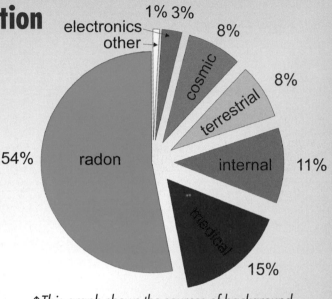

↑ This graph shows the sources of background radiation for an average person.

About half of this radiation (54%) comes from radon in the ground that seeps naturally into buildings over time. Other sources are from medical scans, food, terrestrial building materials, cosmic rays, and electronics like TVs, computers, and cell phones. Other sources that make up less than one percent of the total include radiation from nuclear power plants and radiation from nuclear bomb testing. If a person flies often, smokes cigarettes, or gets extra medical X-rays, he or she will receive more radiation than the average background level.

In some locations in the world, background radiation is up to 200 times greater than average. In these locations, no negative health effects in people have been found. This means that it is possible that some radiation can be good for health, similar to how a vaccine helps a person's immune system recognize and prevent illness.

In 1899 to 1900, Ernest Rutherford and French chemist Paul Villard (1860–1934) discovered the three main types of ionizing radiation. They organized them based on how well they penetrate different common materials. The three types of ionizing radiation are the following:

1) Alpha particles are emitted when heavy radioactive nuclei break up. An alpha particle (whose symbol is the Greek letter α) is made of two neutrons and two protons. Alpha particles are used in smoke detectors, as well as power generators for heart pacemakers and deep space probes.

2) **Beta particles** (β) are electrons with a lot of energy. They come from the breakup of a neutron in the nucleus of the unstable atom into a proton and an electron. Beta particles are used to treat and kill cancer cells, and in PET brain scanners.

3) Gamma (γ) and X-ray radiation are made of photons with very high frequency and energy. X-rays were discovered in 1895 by German physicist Wilhelm Röntgen (1845–1923) when he was experimenting with Crookes' tubes. Gamma radiation is the most energetic type of radiation. It is used to kill bacteria in food, to kill cancer, in security scanners, and for studying deep space.

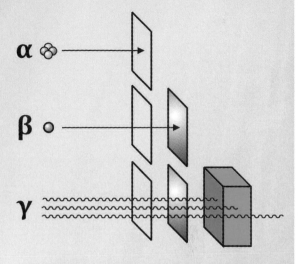

↑ Alpha radiation is easily stopped by thin materials, like paper or skin. Beta radiation is stopped by less than an inch of metal. Gamma radiation is hard to stop even with a thick piece of lead!

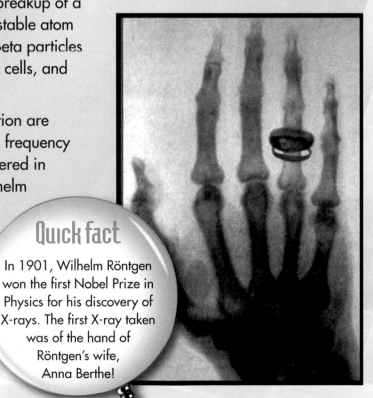

Quick fact

In 1901, Wilhelm Röntgen won the first Nobel Prize in Physics for his discovery of X-rays. The first X-ray taken was of the hand of Röntgen's wife, Anna Berthe!

Making Use of Radiation

Examples of nonionizing radiation include the release of low energy neutrons, photons released as visible light, infrared light, microwaves, or radio waves. Nonionizing radiation is less likely to damage cells, but can be observed in other ways, such as by the light it emits, or by measuring photons of other frequencies with special cameras.

Marie Curie

Marie Curie was one of the most successful experimental scientists of all time. She used the electrometer—a device to measure the electrical conductivity of air, which was invented by her husband and her brother—to measure the level that air near radioactive materials was charged: more for higher radiation and the opposite for lower radiation. In 1898, she and her husband discovered two new elements on the periodic table, polonium (Z=84) and radium (Z=88). Curie was the first woman to be awarded the Nobel Prize, and the first out of only two people to receive two Nobel Prizes (Linus Pauling was the second). She was also the first woman elected to the French Academy of Sciences and the first female professor at the University of Paris.

↑Marie Curie, shown in her laboratory with her husband, Pierre, was a scientific superstar!

The daughter of Marie and Pierre Curie, Irène Joliot-Curie, continued her parents' work. She and her husband, Frédéric Joliot-Curie, discovered that materials that were stable could be made radioactive using a beam of neutrons. For their work, she and her husband won the Nobel Prize in 1935, bringing the Curie family a total of three Nobel Prizes!

Carbon Dating

Natural carbon (C) atoms throughout the universe are made up of two isotopes: ^{12}C with 6 protons and 6 neutrons in the nucleus, and ^{13}C with 6 protons and 7 neutrons. Both are stable and not radioactive. A third isotope of carbon that is radioactive—^{14}C, with 6 protons and 8 neutrons—is made in small amounts by cosmic rays from the Sun in the atmosphere. This ^{14}C then transports to Earth's surface in rain and snow as carbon dioxide, which is food for plants. Those plants are then eaten by animals, giving them a very small amount of ^{14}C in their bodies. This only happens, though, when the organism, either a plant or an animal, is alive. When it dies, it stops taking in ^{14}C.

Because ^{14}C is radioactive, it decreases over time when no new material is being added. This happens in a very predictable way over time and can be measured with sensitive detectors. Using this method, samples of ancient bone, food, wood, or other organic material dug up in archaeological digs can be measured and dated accurately up to about 50,000 years old.

← This photograph shows the modern radiocarbon dating facility at the Lawrence Livermore National Laboratory. This system is about 10,000 times more sensitive than the original method invented by Willard Libby.

CHAPTER SIX

Nuclear Fission and Fusion

Chapter 5 described unstable atoms that become stable by the release of alpha, beta, or gamma radiation. Normally, the particles released from nuclei as radiation make up a small fraction of the mass of the original unstable nucleus. There is one special case that happens to some very large atoms. When they are struck by a single neutron with just the right energy, these atoms will split nearly in half! This process is called nuclear **fission**, and it releases an enormous amount of energy.

Fission is special because in addition to splitting the nucleus into two halves when it is hit by a neutron of the right energy, three extra neutrons are also released at the same time. If these extra neutrons then go on to strike three more nuclei nearby, they may each also fission, releasing more energy and nine more neutrons. These neutrons will then hit nine more nuclei, and so on. Because the reaction helps itself continue without outside help, and will grow quickly in time, fission is called a "self-sustaining chain reaction." This means that when conditions are right, fission will continue by itself as long as there is fuel—nuclei that will fission—nearby.

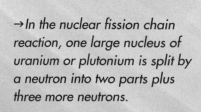

→ In the nuclear fission chain reaction, one large nucleus of uranium or plutonium is split by a neutron into two parts plus three more neutrons.

Two atoms are known to experience fission: an isotope of uranium (U, Z=92, A=235), which is found naturally in 0.71 percent of uranium in the ground, and an isotope of plutonium (Pu, Z-94, A=239). When a nucleus of these materials fissions, it produces one element with an atomic mass of 80 to 100 (for example, strontium, zirconium, and palladium). It also produces another element with an atomic mass of 120 to 160 (for example, tin, iodine, cesium, and barium). Some of these products are radioactive, so they must be handled and stored carefully. In a way, nuclear fission was what the original alchemists like Hennig Brand and Robert Boyle were seeking over 250 years prior to the discovery of fission: a way to transform one element on the periodic table into another.

In 1934, Italian physicist Enrico Fermi (1901–1954) was studying the effect of neutrons on heavy elements. In one test with uranium, he believed he had created a brand new heavier element. Austrian scientist Lise Meitner (1878–1968) and German scientists Otto Hahn (1879–1968) and Fritz Strassmann (1902–1980) began similar tests. With the help of Otto Frisch (1904–1979), they found barium (Ba, Z=56, A=137) in the uranium afterward, proving that a new element had been created by splitting uranium nuclei. Based on this result, Hungarian physicist Leo Szilárd (1898–1964) realized fission could lead to a chain reaction and release huge amounts of energy.

↓ Enrico Fermi was the first person to split the atom using fission.

Putting Fission and Fusion to Work

Knowing that fission could be used to release energy, scientists in the late 1930s worked quickly to build a device that could control the reaction—a nuclear reactor. The first human-made nuclear reactor was called the Chicago Pile-1 (CP-1). It was built at the University of Chicago and started the first chain reaction for 28 minutes on December 2, 1942. The first nuclear power plant began operating in 1951. Today there are over 400 nuclear reactors in over 30 countries producing electricity.

At the same time, research into the use of nuclear fission for weapons was also being done. In 1939, Albert Einstein warned the President of the United States, Franklin Roosevelt (1882–1945), that the discovery of fission could lead to extremely powerful bombs, which the Germans (who had just started World War II) were currently researching. The Manhattan Project then started in 1943 with the purpose to develop the nuclear bomb to win the war. This effort led to dropping the atomic bomb on Hiroshima and Nagasaki in Japan in 1945, ending World War II.

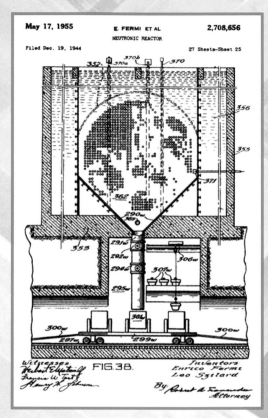

↑ The first human-made nuclear reactor, CP-1, was built under an unused stadium stand.

Quick fact

One pellet of uranium fuel for a nuclear power plant has a mass of 0.57 ounces (16 g). This pellet is able to produce the same amount of electricity as 149 gallons (564 L) of oil, 1,780 lbs (807 kg) of coal, or 17,000 cubic feet (481 m³) of natural gas!

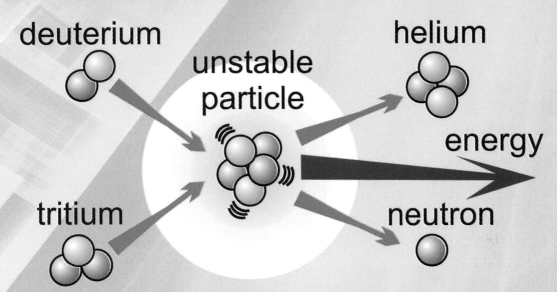

deuterium

unstable particle

helium

tritium

energy

neutron

↑ In fusion, two isotopes of hydrogen (H, Z=1) are joined together to form a helium atom (He, Z=2), a neutron, plus an immense amount of energy.

Where nuclear fission is the process of splitting apart heavy nuclei, nuclear **fusion** is the opposite. In fusion, the nuclei of light atoms like hydrogen are joined together to form a larger, heavier nucleus. When this happens, a staggering amount of energy is released. The fusion of one ounce of hydrogen would release the same amount of energy that is released in the fission of 160 ounces of uranium!

"...what we're going to have to do at a global scale, is create a new system. ...we need energy miracles."

—Bill Gates, founder and chairman of Microsoft

To join two nuclei into one, the original two atoms must have a lot of kinetic— moving—energy. This is because the two nuclei have the same positive charge, and—like two magnets with the same side moved together—will repel each other. When a gas is given this much energy, it heats up to form a plasma, which is the fourth state of matter. For fusion to start, in fact, the plasma has to heat up to about 212,000,000 degrees Fahrenheit (100,000,000°C)! At this temperature, matter tries very hard to expand and cool down. It is the challenge of fusion to hold matter at that temperature and density so that power can be produced from the heat made by the fusion reaction.

Fusion: Power Source of the Future

Australian physicist Mark Oliphant (1901–2000) discovered fusion at the University of Cambridge, England, in 1932. After that, major advancements in fusion were not made until the 1950s, when two main approaches to fusion energy were developed:

1. Magnetic confinement fusion: A donut-shaped (also called a torus) magnetic "bottle" is used to hold plasma in place while heating it. This works well because plasma is made from charged particles, and placing them in a circle means they can be contained while fusion occurs. This type of fusion reactor was invented by Russian physicists Igor Tamm (1895–1971) and Andrei Sakharov (1921–1989) in 1956. They called the reactor a *tokamak*, which is a Russian acronym for a torus-shaped chamber with magnetic coils.

2. Inertial confinement fusion: Great amounts of laser energy are used to squeeze a small amount of hydrogen fuel into helium.

Both approaches are being used by thousands of scientists studying fusion around the world, with the goal of making a fusion power plant in the next 30 years.

Advantages and Disadvantages of Fusion

Advantages
- Fusion is a source of limitless energy.
- Hydrogen fuel for fusion can be found in water! No fossil fuels are used.
- The product of fusion, helium, is not a greenhouse gas, not radioactive, and not polluting.
- There is no risk of the reactor running out of control, so it is very safe.
- A large amount of power can be produced in a small reactor, and it can make power day and night.

Disadvantages
- Fusion is difficult and expensive to achieve.
- Plasma is hard to control, so very fast electronics and control systems must be used to ensure that the plasma does not cool, deionize back to a gas, and stop producing energy.

People Are Made from Star Dust!

Nuclear fusion is the process that powers all of the stars! Stars use gravity to squeeze nuclei together, instead of magnets or lasers like fusion experiments on Earth. The closest star to Earth, the Sun, is a huge swirling ball of hot hydrogen plasma. The Sun is about 864,000 miles (1.4 million kilometers) in diameter, or 109 times the diameter of Earth. The temperature on the surface is about 10,000 degrees Fahrenheit (5,500°C), and at the core—the very center—scientists guess the temperature is over 27 million degrees Fahrenheit (15 million degrees Celsius). It is at the core where light elements fuse into heavier elements, releasing huge amounts of energy.

Our Sun is believed to be a third generation star. This means it was made from matter released as gas and dust after the death of two previous generations of stars. Each successive star generation produces larger atoms by fusion. In later stars, heavier elements burn hotter and produce even heavier elements. Some of the products of fusion in stars that came before our Sun ended up being formed into the planets, moons, asteroids, and comets in our solar system. This means that every atom that makes up Earth, all of nature, and our very own bodies originated in stars billions of years ago.

"Every great advance in science has issued from a new audacity of imagination."

—John Dewey, *The Quest for Certainty: A Study of the Relation of Knowledge and Action,* 1929

↑ *The surface of the Sun is a turbulent mix of plasma and magnetic energy.*

CHAPTER SEVEN

Atomic Theory Today

Studies of radioactivity, fission, and fusion from the 1930s to 1950s were providing important information about the structure of the atomic nucleus. Around the same time, scientists began to change their understanding of matter. Max Planck and Albert Einstein had shown earlier that all photons in the electromagnetic spectrum had a specific frequency, just like waves traveling across water. These scientists had also shown that these photons had energy, which was released in set amounts as electrons in an atom moved to lower energy levels. In 1924, Louis de Broglie (1892–1987) had a theory that the behavior of the electron could also be better understood not just as a particle, but as both a particle and a wave. In 1926, Austrian physicist Erwin Schrödinger (1887–1961) created an equation that described how de Broglie's theory would be possible, not only for atoms and parts of the atom, but even for large objects— maybe even for the entire universe!

Photographing the Atom

In 2009, individual atoms were photographed for the first time by physicists at the Kharkov Institute of Physics and Technology in the Ukraine. Electrons that exist as both a particle and a wave in quantum mechanics are seen as a cloud spread out around the nucleus in a shape known as an orbital. Electrons in two energy levels are shown in the photograph, each with a different shape. The diameter of the electron cloud is about 5.5×10^{-9} inches (1.4×10^{-10} m, or 140 picometers).

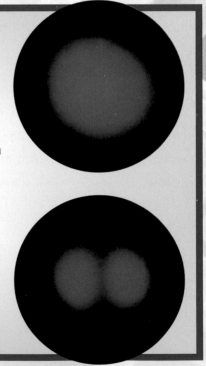

→ The first detailed images of atoms show the electron cloud around a carbon atom.

De Broglie's theory was confirmed in 1929 by George Thomson (1892–1975) of England (and the son of physicist J.J. Thomson who discovered the electron!) and Americans Clinton Davisson (1881–1958) and Lester Germer (1896–1971) at Bell Labs in New Jersey. The three physicists did experiments sending beams of electrons toward small objects. These experiments showed that the electrons did not pass by the objects as particles, but as interacting waves, creating a pattern on the opposite side of the object. In 1945, Ernest Wollan (1902–1984) showed that the same wave-particle theory of matter also applied to neutrons. The theoretical work of Niels Bohr, Max Planck, Louis de Broglie, Albert Einstein, and others made it possible to describe energy and matter mathematically as both a wave and a particle. The quantum theory of matter, also known as quantum mechanics, was born!

The Famous Bell Laboratories

In 1880, Scottish inventor Alexander Graham Bell (1847–1922) founded the Volta Laboratory to study the recording and transmission of sound after his invention of a practical telephone in 1876. In 1925, this laboratory was renamed Bell Laboratories and became the research department of the American Telephone & Telegraph company (AT&T). Since then, research at Bell Labs has led to seven Nobel Prizes and countless innovations in computer hardware and software.

Engineering the Atom

From 1900 to 1930, J.J. Thomson, Ernest Rutherford, James Chadwick, and others had shown that atoms—originally suggested by Democritus to be solid—actually could be divided. The components of an atom—electrons, protons, and neutrons—were called **subatomic particles**, whose size is much less than that of an atom itself. From 1930 to 1960, a number of new subatomic particles were theorized and discovered, which appeared to make atomic theory much more complicated. As a result, scientists began to understand atomic theory in a whole new way.

↑ *The Sudbury Neutrino Observatory (SNO) was built to find neutrinos 1.3 miles (2.1 km) underground. The world's largest neutrino observatory is called IceCube and was completed in December 2010 at the South Pole.*

Nanotechnology

As physicists began to realize atoms were smaller and smaller, engineers developed tools that could explore deeper into, and change, the structure of material at the atomic scale. The name given to this area of science is called **nanotechnology**, which is a reference to the size of the structures being studied: between about 4 and 400 billionths of an inch (1 and 100 nanometers, or 1×10^{-9} and 1×10^{-7} meters). At this scale, materials act differently than they do at larger scales due to quantum mechanics. Research in nanotechnology today includes creating new materials, designing microelectronic parts and advanced computer processors, and designing tiny machines that could be used for electronic or medical purposes.

The idea of the first new subatomic particle came in 1931 when Austrian physicist Wolfgang Pauli (1900–1958) theorized that a second particle was produced when beta particles were created, which had no electric charge and much less mass than an electron. Enrico Fermi named this particle the *neutrino*, finally discovered in 1956. Neutrinos are the most mysterious particles known in the universe. Their exact mass is still unknown. However, at least six types are known, and they travel at close to the speed of light! A great number of neutrinos are produced in the fusion process that takes place in the Sun. Today, however, only about one-third of neutrinos are detected compared to the number expected based on our understanding of the Sun.

Scientists are currently doing experiments to find the missing neutrinos. In 1935, Japanese physicist Hideki Yukawa (1907–1981) predicted there was another type of subatomic particle in an atom's nucleus. The function of this particle was to hold the protons in the nucleus together in a similar way that photons carry electromagnetic energy from one place to another. This force was later called the "nuclear force," and the new type of particle was named a *meson*. In 1947, the first meson was discovered by Cecil Powell (1903–1969), César Lattes (1924–2005), and Giuseppe Occhialini (1907–1993) in England. It was named the "pi" meson, or simply the *pion*. Since then, a total of 140 separate mesons have been identified.

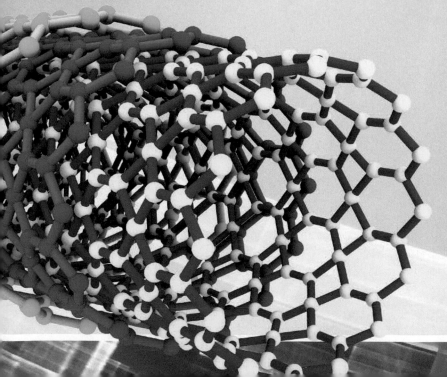

←A nanotube made from carbon atoms is shown. A carbon nanotube is the strongest structure ever made, with over 300 times the strength of the strongest steel and about the same hardness as diamond. If carbon nanotubes could be made in large quantities, they could revolutionize the entire manufacturing industry.

A New World of Subatomic Particles

←A computer simulation of one particle colliding with and breaking up another shows tracks of the subatomic particles that make up atoms.

The next type of subatomic particle was actually discovered before the pion, but its identity was not known at the time. Americans Carl Anderson (1905–1991) and Seth Neddermeyer (1907–1988) discovered the *muon* while also studying cosmic rays. This subatomic particle was almost the same as the electron but was about 200 times heavier. Next, in 1947, George Rochester (1908–2001) and Clifford Butler (1922–1999) of England discovered another charged particle from cosmic ray events that proved to have about half the mass of a neutron or proton. These particles were called *kaons*.

In the 1950s, new technology in particle physics brought more and more powerful **particle accelerators** and more sensitive particle detectors. Using particle accelerators meant that particle physicists could do tests creating subatomic particles without the need to depend on cosmic rays that occur randomly. Another large number of subatomic particles were then discovered, including antiparticles that had the same mass as their counter particle, but the opposite electric charge. For example, the antiparticle of an electron is called a *positron*. When a particle and its antiparticle collide, they join together to form a photon.

In 1964, American physicist Murray Gell-Mann (1929–) and Russian physicist George Zweig (1937–) proposed a theory that most of the new particles being discovered were made up of even smaller particles called **quarks**. They believed that quarks could not be separated further (just as other scientists had believed about atoms until the electron was discovered!). They also believed that quarks came in six different types, or "flavors," plus matching antiquarks that made up the antiparticles. These flavors were named *up, down, strange, charm, top,* and *bottom.*

Using the theory, the properties of each subatomic particle known could be predicted based on it being made of either two or three quarks. Neutrons and protons, for example, were each made of three quarks in a particular pattern. Mesons were made of one quark and one antiquark. Proof of the existence of quarks came just four years later with high-energy experiments at the Stanford Linear Accelerator Center (SLAC) in California. In 1995, the sixth and final quark flavor to be discovered, the *top* quark, was found at the Fermi National Accelerator Laboratory near Chicago, Illinois.

The success of the quark model in describing nature as it was known was thrilling for scientists at the time. By the 1970s, though, an even larger model—the Standard Model—would be developed to bring together our understanding of nearly all particles and forces throughout the universe.

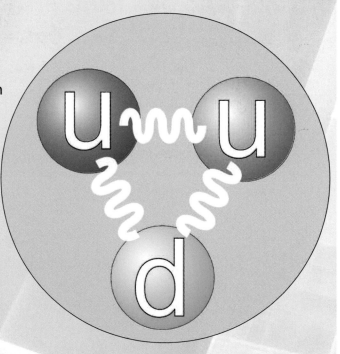

↑ *The proton is made of two up quarks and one down quark. The neutron is the opposite; it is made of two down quarks and one up quark. The quarks are held together by another particle called the* **gluon***, which is shown as a wavy line.*

CHAPTER EIGHT

Cutting-Edge Careers

In 1960, American physicist Sheldon Glashow (1932–) suggested a way to categorize the subatomic universe using a set of laws and theories that describe both matter and energy. He called this set the Standard Model of particle physics. Since that time, the Standard Model has been expanded but has stood the test of time, accurately describing and predicting properties of atoms and hundreds of known subatomic particles in a mathematical way.

↓The Standard Model includes all of the elementary particles that make up matter in the universe.

Today, it is understood that subatomic particles are separated into two groups: those thought to be elementary, and those made from other elementary particles. Particles made from other particles are called *hadrons*, and include protons and neutrons. Elementary particles are also split into two groups: *fermions* and *bosons*. Fermions are particles that make up matter. They include *quarks*, which combine to make hadrons; and *leptons*, which include electrons, muons, and neutrinos. Bosons are subatomic particles that carry forces. The boson family includes photons, particles that hold quarks together called gluons, "Z" and "W" bosons that hold atomic nuclei together, and the last piece of the puzzle, the Higgs boson, which has not yet been discovered. In all, six flavors of quarks, six types of leptons, and five types of bosons are now thought to be the fundamental building blocks of the universe.

fermions			bosons	
quarks				**force carriers**
u up	c charm	t top	photon	
d down	s strange	b bottom	Z boson	
leptons			W boson	
electron neutrino	muon neutrino	tau neutrino	g gluon	
e electron	muon	tau	Higgs boson	

Some of the most challenging and exciting careers in the world today and in the future are in physics. Theoretical particle physicists studying the Standard Model are using the most powerful particle accelerator in the world to search for the final piece of the puzzle, the Higgs boson, which is believed to give all matter its mass.

Theoretical physicists studying string theory are trying to find a "theory of everything," which joins the Standard Model with quantum mechanics.

Other high-energy physicists are searching for particles that have not existed since the beginning of the universe!

Searching for the Higgs Particle at the LHC

The Large Hadron Collider (LHC) is the largest and most powerful particle accelerator in the world. It is located at the European Organization for Nuclear Research (CERN), which is near Geneva on the border of France and Switzerland. The accelerator gives protons seven trillion electron volts of energy so that they move at nearly the speed of light in opposite directions, smashing together and breaking up into subatomic particles. The LHC is the first accelerator that has enough power to break particles into the last missing piece of the Standard Model, the Higgs boson.

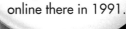

Quick fact

Over 10,000 particle physicists and engineers from 80 countries work at CERN. CERN is also where the World Wide Web (WWW) began. The very first website went online there in 1991.

Careers in Particle Physics, Medicine, and Electronics

Since the first X-ray was taken in 1895, careers in particle physics have also existed in the medical field where scientists have developed ways to look inside the body and treat organs without having to perform surgery. Doctors in hospitals around the world use radioisotopes in nearly 40 million procedures every year, helping to save lives. Starting in 1946, radiation from nearly 200 different isotopes—like technetium (Tc, Z=43) and iridium (Ir, Z=77), all made in nuclear reactors and particle accelerators—have been used to treat cancer and dozens of other diseases.

String Theory

Since the 1980s, scientists have been developing a theory that even quarks and leptons are not elementary but made of smaller parts named "strings." In the theory, strings are one-dimensional objects that, when moving and vibrating together, give matter its mass, charge, flavor, and all of its other properties. String theory would join the Standard Model with the theory of quantum mechanics and gravity so that the entire universe would be described by one grand theory. In the physical world, four dimensions are experienced: three dimensions of space plus one dimension of time. String theory predicts that there are 11 or more dimensions! So far, string theory has not made any predictions that can be tested, but it is hoped that high-energy experiments like the LHC will make it possible to observe the effects of strings.

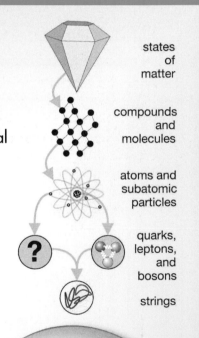

states
of
matter

compounds
and
molecules

atoms and
subatomic
particles

quarks,
leptons,
and
bosons

strings

Quick fact

Five Nobel Prize winners have used atomic theory in medicine, including the use of isotopes to identify drugs and viruses in the human body, and development of the computerized axial tomography (CAT) scan and MRI machines.

With new computers, the entire body can be imaged in three dimensions using atomic theory! The Positron Emission Tomography (PET) scanner, invented in 1961, uses gamma rays to produce positrons—the antiparticle to the electron—which can be imaged in very fine detail. The Magnetic Resonance Imaging (MRI) scanner—invented in 1973—uses a strong magnetic field to align atoms in the body so that they can be photographed.

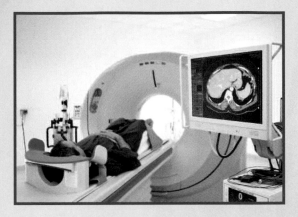

↑An advanced MRI scanner uses a superconducting magnet to view the inside of the body in three dimensions.

Careers in atomic physics are also important for studies of advanced materials and electronics. Microprocessors are now found in every appliance and car, as well as the many pieces of electronics that people use every day. The next generation of processors will be built with electronic features made from silicon that are just 900 billionths of an inch (22 nm) in size. This distance is almost 5,000 times less than the thickness of a human hair, and equal to the atomic radius of just 100 atoms across! To make these processors work, electronics designers need to understand atomic theory, electric and magnetic fields, and the quantum nature of the particles.

↑Nanotechnology will help make new materials possible for the benefit of people all around the world, including faster, more efficient microchips and computer processors.

Careers in Materials, Energy, and Space

An understanding of atomic theory is also needed for the design of advanced materials using nanotechnology. New materials could be stronger and less brittle, and could be used to make everything from new space vehicles, artificial joints for people, longer lasting batteries, stronger building materials and armor, more efficient chemicals used in making new medicines, better ways to use fuels, and faster computers, to name just a few.

Careers in particle physics are also found in energy. Safer, more efficient ways to use nuclear fission are being developed. These devices will be able to make radioactive waste less harmful to people, and to destroy the uranium and plutonium used in nuclear weapons. Atomic theory is also helping to develop new ways to make renewable energy technologies, like solar power, more efficient. Finally, energy from nuclear fusion is on the verge of becoming a reality. Fusion promises to make clean, safe, limitless energy without making dangerous radioactive materials, greenhouse gases, or polluting chemicals.

← *The International Thermonuclear Experimental Reactor (ITER) is now under construction and will start to operate in 2019. ITER will be 10 stories tall and will produce 500 million watts of fusion power!*

"Somewhere, something incredible is waiting to be known."

—Carl Sagan (1934–1996)

→ The Thirty Meter Telescope (TMT) will be the largest telescope in the world when it is finished in 2018. With 10 to 100 times the power of the Hubble Space Telescope, it will help people see much farther into space than ever before.

Finally, careers in particle physics are found in the study of space. Experiments are being performed on the International Space Station (ISS) to study radiation in orbit around Earth and its effects on people. The largest telescopes ever designed are now under construction to help people understand why the universe exists.

"We are at the very beginning of time for the human race. It is not unreasonable that we grapple with problems. But there are tens of thousands of years in the future. Our responsibility is to do what we can, learn what we can, improve the solutions, and pass them on."

—Richard P. Feynman, 1955

Over the past 4,000 years, the nature of the universe has made people wonder, investigate, experiment, and analyze the matter around them. Scientists from all around the world have taken part in a quest to understand the universe built from atoms and subatomic particles. It is now known that the elements, molecules, and forces that can be seen, touched, and tasted are made from atoms, which are made from protons, neutrons, and electrons. Those particles are made from quarks and leptons, which themselves may be made from even smaller strings. Today, the answers to the questions asked by the original Indian and Greek scholars about atomic theory and the nature of matter help people understand where the universe came from, what it is made of, where it is going, and how to make the world a better place for everyone.

Timeline

2000 B.C.–1500 B.C. Water is described as the first element in ancient natural law of India.

900 B.C.–600 B.C. Ancient texts expand elements to five (air, sky, fire, earth, and water).

600 B.C.–300 B.C. Greek philosophers start atomism, suggest everything is made of atoms. Alchemists attempt to change metals into gold.

1676 Light is demonstrated to move at a measureable speed (very fast!).

1704 The universe is thought to be made of solid masses in motion.

1803 Atomic theory is proposed with spherical solid atoms.

1838 The electron is predicted to exist to explain chemical properties of atoms.

1869 Known elements are organized into the periodic table based on mass and properties.

1873 Electric and magnetic fields are predicted to act between atoms.

1895 X-rays are discovered and found to travel through most solids.

1897 Electrons are found, showing for the first time that atoms are themselves made of smaller parts that can be separated.

1898 Radioactivity is discovered.

1900 Gamma radiation is discovered; Isotopes are discovered.

1905 Photons are theorized; mass of a particle and its energy are predicted to be related by Albert Einstein.

1907 Atoms are found to be mainly empty space between the nucleus and the electrons.

1909 Electron charge and mass are measured.

1917 The atom is first split by fission.

1921 Neutrons are predicted to exist.

1922	Properties of photons are demonstrated.
1929	The first particle accelerator ("atom smasher") is built.
1932	Neutrons are discovered; their mass is almost equal to that of a proton.
1942	The first nuclear fission reactor is built.
1951	Artificially-made elements are created for the first time.
1956	The size of the proton is measured for the first time.
1964	Quarks are predicted to exist as the building blocks for protons and neutrons.
1968	Quarks are discovered.
1978	Modern Standard Model of the atom is made.
1979	Gluons that hold quarks together are discovered.
1981	First microscope that sees atoms at the surface of a material is invented.
1989	Individual atoms are moved into patterns.
1990	The Hubble Space Telescope is launched.
1993	First microscope able to see electron clouds is invented.
1996	Hottest plasma temperature is recorded of 936 million degrees Fahrenheit (520 million degrees Celsius).
2005	Atoms are seen moving at different temperatures.
2006	Hottest temperature ever measured is recorded: 6.5 billion degrees Fahrenheit (3.6 billion degrees Celsius).
2009	World's most powerful particle accelerator at CERN (the European Organization for Nuclear Research) comes online. First photos of single atoms are taken. First 3-D image of atomic bonds is made.
2010	Electrons are seen moving for the first time. The size of atoms is measured with lasers.

Glossary

alchemy Ancient practice attempting to change common metals into gold; helped lead to modern chemistry

alpha particle An energetic atom with two protons and two neutrons but no electrons; can easily be stopped by most solids; one of the three main types of radiation

atom Basic unit of matter with a central nucleus in the middle and one or more electrons circling around it

atomism Ancient philosophy that the world is made from two parts, atoms of different shapes and sizes, and empty space between them

beta particle High-energy electrons free from a nucleus; one of the three main types of radiation

cathode An electrical conductor through which an electric current can flow

covalent bond Chemical bond where two electrons are shared to hold two separate atoms together

electric charge Positive or negative property of protons and electrons that makes opposite particles attract, and equal charges repel

electromagnetic spectrum List of all possible photon types based on their energy; includes photons that are radio waves, microwaves, light our eyes can see, and gamma rays

electron Subatomic particle that carries a negative charge, exactly opposite to that of a proton. Without extra energy, electrons circle the nuclei in atoms.

fission Process where the nuclei of large atoms are split into two or more parts, releasing a huge amount of energy

fusion Process where small nuclei are forced to join together, making a new, larger nucleus and releasing huge amounts of energy; used by the Sun and all other stars as a power source

gamma ray The most energetic type of photons; can travel easily through most solids; one of the three main types of radiation

gas One of four normal states of matter. Molecules in a gas are far apart compared to atoms in a solid or liquid, and not charged like in a plasma.

gluon Particle that holds quarks in protons and neutrons together. Gluons have no mass.

ion An atom or a molecule without an equal number of protons and electrons, making it charged

ionic bond Chemical bond between two oppositely charged atoms

isotope Atoms of the same chemical element but with different numbers of neutrons, giving them the same chemical properties but different masses

liquid One of four normal states of matter. Like a gas, a liquid flows and will take the shape of its container, but does not expand to fill a space like a gas.

metallic bond Chemical bond where electrons are shared among metal atoms and can freely move

nanotechnology Studying and making materials on the atomic scale. One nanometer is equal to 39 billionths of an inch (one billionth of a meter).

neutron Subatomic particle that makes up about half the mass of the nucleus of an atom; has a neutral charge, and is made up of quarks

nucleus Central core of an atom that includes protons and neutrons and almost all of the atomic mass

particle accelerator Device that uses strong magnetic fields to create high-speed particle highways (or beams) directed into targets or other beams; also called an atom smasher. Particles are photographed after they break up, helping scientists see what makes up an atom.

periodic table Display of all chemicals known to exist arranged by their mass and periodic properties; contains 118 elements (so far!). Ninety-four are found naturally, while the rest are artificially made.

photon Particle that is the basic unit of light; has no mass; carries energy from one point to another at the speed of light; travels like both a particle and a wave

plasma Fourth state of matter; made when a gas is heated to extremely high temperatures

proton Subatomic particle that makes up about half the mass of the nucleus of an atom; has positive electric charge, and is made up of quarks

quark Building block of protons and neutrons. No smaller building block is currently known.

radiation Motion of energetic particles from one place to another; can cause a neutral atom to become charged. Three main types of radiation are alpha, beta, and gamma.

radioactivity Breakdown of an unstable nucleus by release of radiation

solid One of four normal states of matter; has a firm shape unlike liquids, gases, and plasmas. Atoms in a solid are tightly connected.

speed of light Speed that all types of photons travel at, equal to 186,000 miles per second (300,000 km/s); named the letter c in atomic theory

subatomic particles Particles that make up atoms

X-ray Type of radiation with less energy than gamma rays, but that can travel through most solids in different amounts

For More Information

Books

Gonick, Larry. **The Cartoon Guide to Physics**. Harper Perennial, 1991.

Halpern, Paul. **Collider: The Search for the World's Smallest Particles**. Wiley, 2010.

Kane, Gordon. **Particle Garden: Our Universe As Understood By Particle Physicists**. Basic Books, 1996.

Krauss, Lawrence M. **Atom: A Single Oxygen Atom's Journey from the Big Bang to Life on Earth ... and Beyond.** Back Bay Books/Little, Brown and Company, 2002.

Websites

The Particle Adventure   **particleadventure.org**
Created by the Particle Data Group at the Lawrence Berkeley National Laboratory, this website provides information about quarks, neutrinos, antimatter, extra dimensions, dark matter, accelerators, and particle detectors!

Physics Central   **physicscentral.org**
Explore the exciting world of physics at this website created by the American Physical Society.

Interactions: Particle Physics News and Resources   **interactions.org**
Visit the Interactions.org website to learn all about particle physics from laboratories in North America, Europe, and Asia.

Websites continued

Amazing Space   **amazing-space.stsci.edu/**
Visit this website, created by the Formal Education Group of the Space Telescope
Science Institute's Office of Public Outreach, to learn all about space.

FusEdWeb   **fusedweb.llnl.gov/**
Created by the Princeton Plasma Physics Laboratory, this website explains all
about fusion energy.

NASA for Students   **www.nasa.gov/audience/forstudents**
Learn all about what the National Aeronautics and Space Administration (NASA)
has been up to.

Quark Dance   **pdg.lbl.gov/quarkdance/**
Learn all about quarks at this website, created by the Particle Data Group at
Lawrence Berkeley National Laboratory.

Particle Accelerator Laboratories
Fermilab   **ed.fnal.gov**
The Fermilab Science Education Office has created this website to provide science
education resources and activities.

SLAC   **www2.slac.stanford.edu/vvc/**
Created by the SLAC National Accelerator Laboratory, the Virtual Visitor Center
provides information about particle physics, including accelerators, detectors,
experiments, and history.

CERN   **project-cernland.web.cern.ch**
Visit CERNLand to learn all about CERN (the European Organization for
Nuclear Research).

Index